VI

Ashley Capes

VI

Copyright Ashley Capes ©2017

Cover: Close-Up Books
Layout & Typeset: Close-Up Books

All rights reserved. No part of this book may be reproduced in any form by any electronic or mechanical means including photocopying, recording, or information storage and retrieval without permission in writing from the authors.

ISBN-13: 978-0-9876231-0-2

Published by Close-Up Books
Melbourne, Australia

For Brooke

acknowledgements

Many of the poems in this collection first appeared at *www.ashleycapes.com* but additional pieces also appeared or are forthcoming in the following publications:

westerly, foam:e, tincture, fourW, regime magazine, writ poetry review, verity la, the blue hour and *the grapple annual #2.*

Thanks to the editors of the above publications for their support.

I would also like to thank my loved ones for many years of support and my readers for their patience in the years between releases.

contents

shreds
Beat Hero
two horse race
what you give me
a table set for thousands #4
menu
inevitability
unclasp
river mist
shy to the sun
more slowly
stage show yellow
little red man
sneak into dusk
pink oceans
Campo de' Fiori
slow clap
boat or cloud
each pale song
mercy
old results
worn out
into a tin can
the luxury to dream
becoming thinner
in the ink
there's a camera
secret to weaving
spoons
cars and elephants
stubborn feet

blackened
pips
super-8 sketches
the gaze
t-shirt wars
destined for mud
3885
visiting
frames
thunderclap
in threes
spare room
water-tight
flying buckets
even frogs could be happy
a long yesterday

I

shreds

if you're somewhere beyond
that keyhole
Alice-like maybe
or sleeping so soundly that
the thunder of
my chest collapsing
does not stir you
and if your pin-cushion veins
are the first things to
change
I want to see it
beyond the rustle of bed sheets
and quiet green bleeps
of equipment
so empty of love that they
must
have never been sad,
which isn't to say you haven't made me
happy – Christ no
it means only that their electricity
cannot grow lonely
and that it is never going to be a match for your
lungs

and if you don't wake
for many hours yet
I'll be listening from the kitchen,
my hands like dull spiders
on the cutlery and pots and dials

and I'll be listening
for the moment you stir
so I can smile as you wake
try to be strong
as you have been strong
for me
stronger than the pain
that
like a wretched ghost, wrings out
its song in the whisper
of your bones,
but a ghost you will nevertheless tear into a million shreds
and then release,
each one now thin enough
for the clouds to swallow.

II

Beat hero

the city's bones
have grown too thin
& your cigarette
thinks only of jazz

no-one matches
your wit
& somehow
you stake out new
territory
with each & every handshake

& later, many years later
after the clanging of trains
has stopped

you'll be sure you were happy

& if photographed you will
look just like a Beat hero.

two horse race

whenever I
catch a glimpse of them warming up for another
round of backchat I
feel all the politics run out of me i
n cartoon speech bubbles filled with Z's and I

swear my tongue is now covered i
n revolutionary posters I
add moustaches and generous splashes of red to
them I
see the landscape of Coke and Pepsi
vying for position and I

am sick with the heavy, two-party apathy – thi
s bullshit is like a shovel-blow to the head and I
'm being offered a big fat price-reduction-placebo
ri
ght after and I

hate having no answers because I
like to fix things, even if I

admit, every one of my good intentions i
s more a fleet of oxen-like handymen but I
am determi
ned to set things right as I
trample things instead, well aware that I
move like a lost Stooges routine and so after so
many fai

VI

lures I
stop

and end up making so little noise that I

well suspect my vote and my lines never stirred
the water.

what you give me

how little of you I see now

not your underside
of beer vaults
and bodily fluids
in superslide

not even a lost necklace
with no picture
inside
and engraved
with a date which means nothing
to the water

if I asked you for help
the stone of your face wouldn't shift
even a hairline
and decades later
it would have soaked enough sun to decay

no words scrawled upon your hard body
to lock in time
and no where a hand,
just folded arms like live wires

I drink with you
but you share no stories with me
that you haven't already told
everyone on the block

VI

you have a garden
where there is supposed softness,
the transient perfume
of flowers
or the space between leaves
where there cannot
possibly
be too much sky

but that is where you hide your
severed limbs
and whatever ghosts
the wind sends in

I have tried to reach you there
where strong veins converge
and everyone passing
has their own tricks to try upon you;
sweet eyes
high scarves
and the immortality
of portraiture

and yet your poses
are never of design
you are just
that colossal
that indifferent

a chameleon

whose dance steps
come with thunder
such that whatever you say is final

I am always watching you

waiting
for that cloud burst

yet you won't even have me wipe
my feet
at the door, I know

since you make it clear
with each thin dawn
that there is nothing I can do for you.

III

a table set for thousands #4

there used to be poetry in my neighbours

the kind
that wasn't meant for me
but could nonetheless leap fences
in a single bound

all struggle used to be poetic too
but now
I wonder if it isn't merely
precursor to defeat

I see it in every pen stroke
and every crossing guard,
even the cobwebs now
seem tired
as the wind cuts into them

in place of the old shop that used to sell
music
there's another $2 store

and I have to wonder if I'm interested
in that sort of future

because it has such slippery fins
you know

and I still want to make poetry
that brings you mercy

VI

and so how impossible it is for me now

to find satisfaction
in my own words
fearing that they heal absolutely
nothing.

menu

up the back
and not quite hidden by the menu
his voice is an idling engine
until he orders again, broken crockery for lips
as he grinds words out
for the girl at the counter
who's waiting for a tip
with miniature scarecrows for her hair
and an expressionless distaste
that rattles mugs, catches in the fan
then falls across us
with the feathery touch of a sigh.

inevitability

new frost ices the fields

and my footprints crunch
and my breath
ghosts

at the fence post
there's so much of empty beyond

even the grass
must be wondering
what happened
where did everyone go?

and there's no answer
beyond the inevitability
of decay

which has long crept up
on us
right down
to the laces of our boots
and the fraying of sincerity

and as I leave

the car becomes a bull
and chews on the road
black bits

getting
stuck between its teeth.

unclasp

rain turns buildings into long pale ghosts
with blocky faces

and clocks grow heavy,
even the lemon trees do not unclasp their fruit

every cloud has to be cut free
from stony carvings of sky

they fall to the grass and smother it in a dew
that cannot be tasted –

and I know if I stand at this window
and watch too long I will never be warm again.

river mist

adjusting
white blankets

the pelicans
fly in pack

big mouths
firm

over
river mist

the sun
at their backs

as they race my car
into morning.

shy to the sun

in a field of yellow grass
fine as thinning hair

the trees have stripped off

their grey bones are shy
to the sun

and the green things inside

no longer shiver
they are dark and blue

as hummingbirds
grown still.

more slowly

months tend to rush through the calendar
with a certain perverse glee

I can hardly keep up
since the days, they flash like streaks of paint
hurled from moving cars

I'm left fumbling with small change
head like a weather-vane in a storm

and you say

slow down

in the hush that follows
I see

little birds filling powerlines
soot
against the new lemon
of the sunset.

stage show yellow

cicadas play back-to-back sets
eventually
emptying their entire bodies of music
and when nothing but the shells remain
the wind comes to tickle them

I walk a town sweltering
beneath yellow gels
like a stage show set in Mexico
with dogs sticking to their water bowls
and policemen in the ice-creamery

and no-one can move without
sweating
no-one wants to talk at all really
and so we pass like liquid robots
all looking for a new sound:

the hush of ice
whispers in the shade
or the splash of a long river
bending back
into a blue miracle.

little red man

tonight the city air shrinks my lungs
and its concrete hates my feet

none of the taxis seem to have eyes
and the drunks scent-mark their pubs
with vomit and cigarette butts

no night-birds bother with music
and the pedestrians
leap forth, as if daring the little red man
in the box to jump down
and take them on. he doesn't

of course

and they live another night.

with nothing better to do, it seems
I keep walking my slow steps

and my legs become skyscrapers,
towering over the vague gravesites
of punished insects

until finally the bus stop looms
like a steel and Perspex umbrella,
ever-ready to save me from
the coming rain.

sneak into dusk

two drunk kids
make their way across the bridge
each step
its own odyssey
laughter
echoing like a couple
of gunshots

startling
pelicans and their briefcase bills

as streetlights
report for service
on
in a
white-hot
blink

and cars sneak into the dusk
their sleek bodies
always
modelling

leaving behind only
a *swish*
and
the taste
of young envy.

pink oceans

here he goes
the boy
into the fairground
now
spitting, kicking spinning
bleeding
words
new words
little angry
fire-cracker words,
he's trying them on
with squeaks
and bright fists
those words
the ones
that belong to others
with bigger hands
workman-like
hands
hands of dark
grease and hair
and thumbnails
huge
moons setting
into their pink oceans
and all gone to hardness
now with the snarl of steel
and blooming fire
all forging
all holding

VI

the usual panic
and promises
but mostly just holding
all the rage
he's trying to copy
down there
by the teacups
spinning their blue handles
into the night
as he paces
and plans
the crack of each word
hitting skin
and the hiss
of every syllable
cutting deep.

IV

Campo de' Fiori

I chase you through the file extensions
littered across my computers
and with each little
click
you are enlarged
but I get no closer, salt in a wound
as the pixels
run
and I hit that X again
only to repeat the whole game
the next night,
in an aching chair
where moths are on loop
and the counterfeit moon
flickers
from inside the light shade,
it seems
now
that whenever I blink
you slip between the frames

and even in memory you fragment
as if the wind had been everywhere first:

gone

the taxi driver's face
but not his cigarettes
         gone

the rainbow of fruit but not the sun
where it punished Bruno's hood
and gone
the hundreds of cats
yet not the graffiti
worming
its way across yellow walls
                              gone
the tourists
but never the things we worshipped.

slow clap

in photographs of me
in the canals
my face eating the sunlight
I smile
because
it's amazing
in my memory
and even now that
winter is heavy
upon us
I somehow forget
wanting to push
my fellow tourists
into the green
and simply get on with
taking comfort
from once, years ago now
once, being so far out
of reach
and no longer
thinking of jackets
thick socks
or desperately
hot showers,
just the slow clap
of feet on dry stone.

boat or cloud

the road slithers into hills
lined with awful
plastic and paper breadcrumbs
before flinging the car
up against the ocean view,
a line of silver and blue
unbroken by any boat
or cloud

houses have been
deposited on the cliffs
like white pieces
on a mountain-range-chessboard,
each move taking years
and years to complete

on the other side is Amalfi
stuffed full of buses
and sipping at the water,
lemon cream and refrains
from the *Tarantella*,
the bubbles in its cafes
racing one another
up the glass.

each pale song

your hair has grown deep
into the green stone of age

just as hills have grown between us
and oceans salt everything –
sunbathers
and their pastel umbrellas
get away with nothing here

and driftwood piles
in hours
heaped upon
what few memories I have gathered

even as my head spills them
in a dance of clouds,
torsos thin,
each pale song
a gouge in my chest

but it is simple enough:
I want you

and now the statues have turned all
shoulders
tear-drop smooth

and the polish of feet
across your body,
how many is it now?

your hands were so wide,
as if to rival Atlas
who was always just out of sight
who was slowly unfreezing
and whose pulse
was seismic
but who could not fit you
within his stern gaze

and I will forgive every stumble
each scratch
each sour bite you give
when ignored
and even, envy so great
as to rattle my very bones

but you hid so well,
caught,
suspended
between a breath
and the settling of night

your sweet face

I wonder
did you ever truly need to paint it?

your own voice grew young
in my listening
and
I leant against cool railings
and you called me back to see
secrets
that were everyone's
but became ours
by the whispers I couldn't fully unearth,

VI

as crowds of automated eyes
pillaged you
as I myself would later do
as so many could not resist to do
and what I kept
could never satisfy

your immortality dried
as we worked,
great deserts in our fingertips
and dust in our kisses

and though I cannot feel more shame
knowing that I want more

at least when change came
thank god
you were not part of its neon creeping.

mercy

linked by the bright blue of our lanyards
we form a kind statistically-varied
'blue team' tour group,
and into the Colosseum
separated only
by the distance of radio signal
and frequency of camera clicks
we go

climbing smooth stone
and moving through arches
passing brickwork
stripped down to its skeleton
by centuries of looters
whether Papal in nature
or committed earlier by dark-agers
desperate for brass

yet it's so easy to forget
smog-stains on the tiers
to look beyond
restoration scaffolding
where it clings like clumsy spider webs

and let my tour group fade,
let the great age of the place
overwhelm –
as so often in this city
I find myself completely
at the mercy of its echoes.

v

old results

    habit closes over my wrist
                                    stay put
    leans hard
    drives itself into my ribs
    and with every white kiss
    every greasy transaction
                        I pay   I eat
            and pay again
    and ask myself
    what else can I cover up
    with all this chocolate?

    god, what barren wonderland
    have I stumbled into now,
    feet stirring dust
    on bones

    they push free
    from the sand like pathetic flags
    in a long frontier, where everyone has
    been before me
    with monster-truck prams
    heavy with sympathy in their wheels
    and tiny laughter
    that ghosts over the sides
                          to flutter
              down
    and settle   finally in my gut
    where it quickly grows comfortable
    and spreads long claws.

worn out

Jesus
how we've almost never talked
except in
confessional
poetry

where I really add nothing
to the genre

but still throw about
aloof
or
hesitant questions

and I don't know how desperate
it is for a confused
prayer
to escape
thin lips

but here we are

the omnipresence of your father
circumventing
any need
for telephone
or ground to cloud
at a discount

and I've got to be sure before I ask
myself
this

does our conversation
now
amount to taciturn
belief
or is it habit
and literary tradition

giving you such agency

and see
how I've stopped short of blame

because life is rough enough
without those good old thunderbolts

and so maybe
this discussion is nothing more
than sorting scars

and obviously
you mirror them

and you're worn out too

but still,
I get the picture

and in you, I will
say at last
what I have fought
long
not to say

VI

simply

that I fear now
surely only fools ever believe in fairness.

into a tin can

a home
in the silks of grass
with fresh tar
on estate roads
too new
to have had
even a single innings
played upon them

streetlights go snapping on
and I'm still trailing
Goliath's finger
across a map of Europe

we say to one another
we'll just work harder
but there's
such slow terror in staying put

I peel another banana
and kick off the same
sequence
of tin-can surprises

I don't want to leave the house
anymore

and when it rains
no-one can collect a single drop,

VI

everything
scrambles in gutters
and when they cross the fields,
even rainbows
tangle
in barbed wire.

the luxury to dream

there are tiny suicides
in day to day living

when you say 'no'
to this or that, when you
chink the curtain
and close the lid
on a dream
so young, so foetal
that no-one
would have any idea
it was even on the horizon,
no idea
that it could have
whispered in the passage of cloth
over skin, and when you
close it away
shove at it with a heartbeat
like a broken down car

you know you must do so
with a firm hand,
because to let it take even
one
gasp of air
would be to give it such purchase
that even a leech
would slither and writhe in envy.

becoming thinner

my fingerprints trail through air
between fence posts, kitchen benches
and car doors; with every step
not even an imprint
left behind
just the barest swish
like lace falling over a window

but
tense up
now
they'll be back with their filthy spoons
soon enough

and I can see the round table now
the lampshade
is stretched with my skin
           and the bulb
spews the red of my heart

I can see their faces now
the expectation, the need   twitching   in
their fingernails
they want a piece
it's going to be heaven for them
and whatever's left I think I can keep
in a child's piggy bank
with
all that

amazing pink,
which you will have to admit is better
than what I've got now

the death-rattle of little coins
in a tin

and every single one of the ghouls
wanting a few cents more
with which to pick clean their teeth.

in the ink

every place is a hotel –

the grind of heels on a gravel driveway
swallowed by wind

a new chip in old furniture
soon lost to dust

maybe the concrete slab too
when the house is torn down

maybe the ash we spread across the winter sky
blown to blue
in spring
and even the holes
we make in things
after each bitter set-back,
will grow moulded over with platitudes

every mark we make is temporary –

a rose petal will rot and stain
smooth kitchen bench-tops
and windows bear the fog
of constant screaming

yet when we leave and everything is cleaned
no thing is porous enough
to snag even an echo of our dreams

those things we thought might endure
but which
now drift between stops on a folded map
like ghost-trains in ink.

there's a camera

on me
must be that – I'm in a pretty bad
film

otherwise why
would I run?

only the same guy
waits beyond the hotel door
carpet spotted
same guy
over the counter
with milk, waiting to buy petrol
same guy
at my desk, typing
shoulders gargoyled
and sure as hell the same guy
in the car park
eating my lunch
desperate for just ten minutes
to himself
stereo on window
cracked
and the same guy still,
at home
not nearly sleeping enough
hands myopic
making their tiny
strikes

and so why else run
such a futile line?

the same guy
is always waiting.

secret to weaving

I have slept without
even a single scrap
to call dream

I have remembered
so little of my childhood
that I might as well
have been a cabbage patch kid

instead

I have looked forward
to things that may
or may not be taken
from tomorrow

I have stopped
at imaginary docks
and cupped dark water

I have combed
silver thread from thistles
in ragged fields

but

never known the secret
to weaving

and instead

it seems

built my home
upon a splice in time

instead been too quick
to shore up the gaps
with greying hands.

spoons

I want more for you –

more than medicine's
many-coloured pinwheel of side effects

like the shittiest fucking game show ever

give us something better than
nausea, migraines, depression
and
a dampening of symptoms
like the drip from an air-conditioner
pooling
in a rat-shit alley

give us more than appointments
to make other appointments
and the stab wounds of the bills that go with them
as red blooms
in vase after vase of plastic flowers

until all I can see is red

because there's yet another test for you to endure
simply
so the resistance of flesh to needle
might be measured again

or the effectiveness of radiation blocking gear,
that too

as we hit our maximum dose for the 12-month
period

I want more for you than I can give

and I know *it's no-one's fault*
a phrase that's like a prayer around here

but I know also, there's no medicine
no magic, no lottery for the things I want for you

classic things like:

routine
surety
looking ahead
the blessing of choice

little mongrels of things people couldn't give a
fuck about
until they're taken away and replaced
with glittering
consolations:

plan B
plan C
plan D
plan E

and on until we achieve true stasis just like
the bikini girl's smile

VI

I want for you something better
than my powerlessness

I want to give you my spoons
as many as I can spare

I want to give you daylight without pain

a week where no gongs sing out new, bizarre symptoms
phoned in from the executive producer
on the top floor

a day where you can simply run again!

criss-cross a park like a giddy butterfly

or maybe swing a racquet

maybe stand
maybe just be able to stand without
having to stand on daggers

or forget

forget

if I could give you a day at least, one day
where you didn't have to know
this is forever.

VI

cars and elephants

in your shadow there is a skeleton
that cooks us dinner
then quietly goes away

it wipes milky bones on the mat
and leaves a clicking sound
lingering   fluttering
down
to meet the damp,
where it waits like a cheek

pressed against a coffin

and as I sit back on the couch
I recede, like Judy spinning
down those yellow bricks,
her doped-up face
brittle with MGM's delight

I think there are cars and elephants
stuck inside of us
                stuck
at intersections, broken down
caught, headlights humming
skin glowing
and pushing, expanding, slowly, expanding
tusks now caught

as the caterpillar turns.

stubborn feet

how you have poisoned yourself
with stubborn
rat feet

scraping each minute
from the sky
and turning for applause
that rung out years ago

you dance the wet mop
of history into a gene pool
laced with crocodiles

they are so patient
their stone heartbeats can clink
to the tuneful
wheezing
of father time

and so when your toe dips in
and their eyelids scatter you

the butterfly net will break the sound barrier

you will finish up
by eating their wings
and spreading the leftovers
across your home

VI

and later steer yourself toward flowers,
those metaphorical mascots
for seizing the day

and wonder if any day could truly
be squeezed into shape.

blackened

walking, sinking a little into the hockey field
& there's a sudden
sense of you
as if I've been jabbed by a pin

it *is* like a death, you know

like you're gone
evaporated into the tiny bits of memory
that remain
after I shake myself
&
the big parts
fall out
to dive through the air

crash into the gutters
& dissolve
like leaf membrane
shivering
beneath a thousand boot heels
as all their scuffs
& skips
& rubbery indifference
finish you off

you left an uncertain spectre
cold breath
dampening my shoulder as I type

VI

& I cannot say now
if I love words
or the world they fabricated

& the seconds between then and now
are growing awful
as they reverberate
& strain
& blacken any
common ground between you and I.

pips

tomorrow is a plum
skin cool to touch

but when I get there
it has rotted down to an eyelash

and the wind snickers
and all of the parking metres turn away

and it rains until
gutters overflow with old wedding dresses
sequins shouting

and the windows flap their shining wings
as the sun comes out

and I see washing cross pastel buildings on string

every drip
hurtling to a hungry street
where the dust grows

until one day only corpses
are left to sift through the pips.

super-8 sketches

how disappointing to remember so little.

my mind can sketch anything in a saturated
super-8 flashback style but only for a few days
and months and years later the picture won't
have any detail at all,
no close-ups
or sense of movement
and at best the soundtrack will be like a pretty
good cover band
and at worst
you won't even recognise the instruments

and no way, if you're looking to pause
something
don't bother, mate
since every frame just sort of floats off into ink
no matter which limb you press

and I miss the things
I used to think were mine

too many of my clips
are just gone
now, time chewing on them like an earthworm
working through pasture,
in through the eyes
and out the back of my head or something,
dissolving

dreaming dying
or already passing
in the chill of winter soil

and the deeper I dig
the thinner everything gets
until all the colour goes too
and my hands are buried in their manyfold deaths.

the gaze

it was noir or pornography
or both
the way the camera
took hold of her
legs and arms
and just took its time
sliding focusing
becoming
until I was fooled
into thinking I was there
but of course
the cinema was murmuring
the whole time
popcorn hissing
and the shivering
of teenage promises
lingering in the seats
so no, I wasn't there
but that big window
still led right to her lips
still gave up
its contrivances
with such a wink
that we all knew exactly
what we were supposed
to be thinking.

t-shirt wars

some parts of a gig
are always the same:

it's easy to see them
preparing early, like me,
flicking through a library of t-shirts
for the one that will ensure
maximum cred

& so at *Them Crooked Vultures*
there's a range to rival that of any pirate's stall

from Nirvana to Kyuss, to Qotsa
& Zeppelin, & even one featuring
Hunter S. Thompson's
receding hairline & trusty
cigarette holder, or the ultimate
trump card, the Zeppelin shirt so faded
that it endows upon the wearer complete
superiority

but some of the shirts make me proud too

worn by guys & girls with no idea
about the standard of warfare
or maybe they were gleefully snubbing it
with flat, no name brands
or even a polo from work,
complete with logo
& name sewn over the breast.

destined for mud

1.

there is a pulse
beneath this state of mind:

like a giant squid biding time
gills very patient
beneath water awfully black
and having melted softly

the car rolls to a halt.
through the trees no more than
a minute of light and then
headlights are clicked off

deep coffee sipped
from the dashboard
a spot of rain

as rats cross leaves
and an owl falls in white,
soundless as the samurai's blade
or the kiss for a sleeping
child's forehead.

the hammer jumps from the boot
and shoes go unpolished
that morning,
destined for mud in any case.

2.

now the engine
with its Tom Waits voice
heading back, flinging
dead animals
into collection-plate-ditches
beside the road

their funerals microscopic

and the speed-dial clock
glowing nuclear,
somewhere in the AM.

later, the raincoat is hosed down
behind a petrol station
with bright lights and sliding doors

in the glove box there is no such
hope.

3.

the wheels hardly blaze
and the handle
to wind the window down
bears a film of sweat

something interferes
with the dusty, country-death song
on the radio

and red sirens echo beneath clouds
that gobble constellations
like ugly worms

VI

from the back seat
something stirs beneath a towel,
gurgles with love
or curiosity
and it makes no difference
to his rattlesnake eyes.

VII

3885

the clothesline
swings
in a dry wind

and the echo of our voices
runs
down from the river
to where I stand
in yellow grass
eyes fixed
on a horizon swollen with blue

the river
where we'd swim
through the black gold of the water
rapids
gnashing teeth
and water dragons
nimble
as we give chase

how sharp the bite
of the sun
who we would
more or less
worship for the entire season
no sand too hot
no bike seat too hard
no hole too far

and nothing
nothing
coming
even close
to lasting long enough.

visiting

maybe that was happiness – murky, unclear and unreliable but bright enough to blind me to tomorrow, before tomorrow became more than I could fit into my pockets. when it was enough for a breeze simply to make the clothesline creak, I'd roll from the concrete path onto soft grass – all grass was soft to a young boy – and the scent of hewn earth would creep across me. there, yellow fibreglass could splay sunlight across the back step, dust motes in a spinning gold rush.

it was always summer; the neighbourhood stray accepted any food we left out. the highway was a nascent thunder.

> tomorrow thin as rumour
> my life a tiny bullet
> as I ricochet off everything

frames

Wiegenlied comes on the radio
and I become a dry crib

pale hands wave – almost
beautiful
the way their lovesick frames
blend with the trees
and give each other
some measure of comfort

as if the entirety of tomorrow
was again assured
and smooth as a passing
wingtip.

thunderclap

I do not have you
except in the half-dream
squeezed between a lunch break

and the next class
where you are asking me
to lift you up
onto my shoulders

who knows exactly
what colour your hair

or whether it would be winter
with frost lurking on bench seats

or whether I would
be gentle enough

and who knows
if I am writing this to naught
but a heroically white cloud
or whether you'd be
hiding in the coming spring

I cannot plan for your small steps

each a thunderclap
in my chest.

in threes

is the possibility of you nothing more
than a bubble
glistening in sunlight?

how quickly I must move

how quickly I must reach and snatch and twist
as if unlocking a dream from a jar –

after which I will spread it across my chest
let it sink into my heart
and wait there, give the strings a good tug

so cherubs might come tumbling
in an avalanche of wings
and rosed cheeks

but instead
comes the reaper, with gentle,
crumbling face and
measured, stately pace

and everything then falling out of focus
around his wingless shoulders
and no fuss, no ruckus
no sounds
no, not even a mouse

as his fingers reach out

VI

and suddenly I am no longer playing with you
the way I used to imagine. I can no longer
protect you
from beestings
and the hard laws of adults,
let you sing whenever you like

now
I am no longer holding you when you sleep

no longer can I wheel loads of wood
from the chopping block to the house
as you help, twigs in hand
and see your little gumboots with
pictures on them
where mine are sober black.

spare room

we'll call it the 'spare' room instead, I guess
there
where absence is found
and we'll both understand
that it's not empty truly

we take out the picture-books
and the little plastic toys
without specific names
– just toys really, some cheap, some cute
and all to be sealed in a larger
plastic coffin
and stuffed between other boxes
and tubs in the shed,
where we don't have to feel the same slice
each time our eyes slide across it

and what I think I'll leave behind
must be more than bitterness
or vicious, thin things that aren't quite prayers
or accusations
but instead, the hush of half-formed promises
I can later make to you face to face –
the idea that two is enough
and was never, not once, ever
                              not enough.

VIII

water-tight

when I used to exhale
a slow stream of cherry blossoms would follow
but now I hold my breath

everything has to be water-tight

no Houdini's allowed
not even one
sweet drop
can fall between
parked cars
where the city stands, grid-locked down to its very bones
its great silver tubes
injecting tired little suits
into the suburbs
and the chaff of their day abandoned;
newspapers with unfinished crosswords
thin, chewing-gum wrappers
and the stale memory
of coffee
flowing between eye-teeth

you are on the other side of it all
I know

as I sit
bound to a green-painted steel bench
glaring at the clock

VI

and its clumsy, digital face

and wonder
if hours will shrink into mere moments
if I just be still and think of you.

flying buckets

after filling the city with water
the storm eases
and winds its way here, less insistent
and entirely willing
to rest between outbursts

we can talk between them if we want
but there's nothing much to say
and that's just fine
for now
as you watch the lightning
and I watch you.

even frogs could be happy

she lifted a lady-of-the-lake
arm to rub
at smudges on sky
until it was clean again and the business
of rain was finished

and all the ponds were full
and frogs could be happy
and I was jealous of them

for just a short time
until she told me soothing things
and I slept on the couch
before sunset
and woke with stars tapping
their silver fingers
on the window

and then she was gone
and the house seemed to sag
with her absence.

a long yesterday

the train clicked over sizzling rails when
I saw you in tall grass

a pink dress

speeding away

I saw you and thought of home

where the border was softer
and where you could slip into a long yesterday

               what a hole a dream leaves

I was a hawk as God's arrow
my feathers left vapour trails

and far below
in the cobblestone square the shopkeepers smiled
and nodded and rested

and when we met
there was a heroic shiver of butterflies within me

leaves were always fluttering
            – you moved and I moved

the bones in your hand sung beneath flesh.

Also by Ashley

pollen and the storm
stepping over seasons
orion tips the saucepan
between giants/old stone
7 years

See more poetry at Ashley's website:

www.ashleycapes.com

or follow him on Twitter:

http://twitter.com/Ash_Capes

www.ingramcontent.com/pod-product-compliance
Lightning Source LLC
Chambersburg PA
CBHW030604020526
44112CB00048B/1213